The Cussing Pastor

Bullsh*t From the Pulpit

Thaddeus Matthews

ISBN-13: 978-1-7366962-0-0

Publisher's Note

Dedication

This book is dedicated to the memory of the two women that made me what I am today, Mable Lee Jordan and Mollie B. Matthews. Even though both of these women have transitioned, their teachings made me bold and courageous.

Mable, my mother, was a cusser with no limits and was known to bluntly put offenders in place.

Mollie B. Who raised me taught me the merits of hard work and the meaning of not giving up. Both these women taught me to never give up or to back down and accept when I'm wrong.

I've spent my life in church and around church leaders I've seen the corruption of this group, including the misinformation being taught. For this reason, there is no better voice to speak on Bullshit From The Pulpit than me.

I hope this book makes those two old ladies proud and may their spirits stand beside me as I stand up for what I know is right.

Pastor T.

1
Allow Me to Introduce Myself

Now, before I start telling you my business, let me explain a few things. See, you have to know where I've been to understand who and where I am, and where I'm headed. There's a lot more to The Cussing Pastor than just cussing motherfuckers out. I've been through some real shit – some funny shit, some serious shit, some trifling shit, some good. Understanding that I'm more than just a man who uses profanity when he speaks or preach the word of God and does whatever the fuck he wants to do. I believe this will change how you perceive me. If it doesn't, fuck it! I hope that you can look past the cuss words and see the man, see the message. Because behind and underneath the cussing, it's one in there.

So, who is The Cussing Pastor?

Well, I was born on April the 1st, 1957. People think I'm joking when I tell them this, but it's true. And He picked the perfect day for me to make my entrance into the world. Yeah, God has a sense of humor. He knew I'd be a damn fool! I grew up in Memphis, Tennessee, in a little area in North Memphis called new Chicago. My mother was 16-

years-old when she had me. Her name was Mable, and she lived with my great-grandmother, Willie Laster, and my grandaunt, Mollie Matthews. I was born Thaddeus Augustus Jordan. After deciding that it would be best for my aunt Mollie to raise me, they changed my last name to Matthews.

Although my mother didn't raise me, I still had a relationship with her, so she was often around. That made it easy for me to get to know my other siblings. My mother was being fast, and she had four more kids after me. Family members also adopted my siblings, but we still stayed in contact.

I did not know my father. I didn't even question fatherhood at that age. There wasn't a need for me to ask about his absence because, in my mind, I had a good life. I never went without anything that I needed. I never experienced poverty, so I didn't know some of the plights of some of the kids that I grew up with.

My aunty was an entrepreneur, so I had no deficiencies as a child. There was no financial struggle because my aunt was the owner of the first black beauty and barber supply in Memphis. It was called Matthews Beauty and Barber supplies. She was a cosmetologist. She did hair, and she sold her own products. We had nice furniture, a colored TV, a washer and dry; we had all of those things that showed how successful my aunt was. She was definitely what this generation now calls the Rich Aunty.

Seeing my aunt work so hard, I naturally followed suit. She would have me tag along with her to all of the black beauty and barbershops in the Metro Memphis area. She would do her thing, and I'd be taking mental notes. I'm grateful that my aunt included me in her journey of entrepreneurship. I learned to follow my passion early on from watching her, which I believe is another reason why I didn't question anyone about my father. Hell, I was living my life. I didn't inquire about him until I was in my late teens, seventeen or eighteen.

Although my biological parents didn't raise me, I'm not mad, upset, or bitter about it. Not being raised by biological parents might affect most people, but not me. I was surrounded by so much love and attention, the lack of theirs didn't faze me one bit. Since I never met my father, I had no one, in particular, to be mad at. I wasn't angry at my mother, either. I knew who my mother was, but she wasn't involved in my day-to-day life growing up. And with my mother and I being so close in age, it was as if we were sister and brother whenever I did see her.

My family structure taught me the difference between a mama and a mother. A mama is a woman who raises, nurtures, provides for and is present in a child's daily life. A mother is a woman who gave birth to a baby. No disrespect to Mable, but my great-grandmother was my mama until she died. And then my aunt, who was TT, became a mama to me. Despite my family structure, I still honor Mable by referring to her as my mother because we still had a bond. It was a unique bond, the kind that most wouldn't understand, but it was our bond, and I'll always love her because of that.

When my great-grandmother died, it was just me, my aunt, and the dog that lived in the house. I was her only heir, and she treated me like so. Some would probably think that I was spoiled, but that was just the way of life for me. My aunt never gave birth to children, which is why she probably was such an incredible guardian to me. She raised me and my mother, who was her sister's oldest child. So I guess that was her motherhood position. That's what she was born to do. Nurture the children that came through her bloodline.

My aunt raised me with so much love. She taught me everything that I knew as a child. And I don't feel any way about it other than gratitude. She could have left my black ass somewhere in the system after my great-grandmother died. But she took me in, loved me, and continued to love my mother and my other four siblings. No, I can't complain at all.

2

Accepting "The Call"

I know you're probably wondering, how in the hell did this man become a pastor? Well, it was predestined. I was created to preach the word of God in an unorthodox way – even though I didn't want to. When my mother was carrying me, a woman named Electra Miller Stewart proclaimed to my aunt and my mother that she was carrying a preacher in her womb. Well, I heard the story, and that was something I had no plans to make come true! My family did because they made sure I was in church all the time. I was faithfully in the Ebenezer Missionary Baptist Church's pews under the tutelage of the late Dr. E. L. Slay. Most folk only go to church on Sundays. Some go to bible study or prayer service once out of the week, and then there are the CME attendees. You know, Christmas, Mother's Day, and Easter. Well, that wasn't my reality. I was in church a minimum of three times a week. I was in Sunday School, the eleven o'clock service, the three o'clock afternoon service, and even the night watch service for many years. I was very biblically trained. I was taught how to stand in a room filled with strangers and speak. I knew how to sing, so I sang in the choir and participated in all the youth programs. Even though I was raised in the church and learned a lot about life, I knew that this was prophesied about me - I still didn't want to be a pastor.

I've heard many times growing up that all preachers hear a voice calling them to become a preacher. These people have said they heard a voice at night confirming that they should be preaching. That's straight bullshit! They're not hearing any voice telling them to preach. It's telling them to go pee! In all seriousness, for me, there was no voice waking me out of my sleep to preach the word of God. But I did find myself under a compulsion to preach. So I did.

I was unsure about becoming a preacher because I knew that my mind didn't work as the average preacher. See, I knew as a small child that I wasn't like everyone else. I knew that I wasn't normal. That only confirms what people say about me now. I understood very early on that there was a special assignment in my life. When I was a small child, I even understood that I would die tragically from something that I'm fighting for or something that I believe in when my time comes. So, yes. I think that I was supposed to preach. I just didn't want to.

At any rate, I accepted what the church refers to as 'the call to Ministry' around 1976. I left Ebenezer, and I became a member of the United

Baptist Church. I preached my first sermon in '76 on the fourth Sunday in December. I was licensed the next month and ordained the following year.

Time was approaching when I'd have to prove my gift to more than just my church home. Word spread around the country that I was a good preacher, and I started getting invited to preach at other churches. Back then, all of the churches wanted to have a young preacher in their pulpit, especially if they had a Youth Ministry. It was a drawing card for them. Since I was youthful and good at what I did, I was speaking everywhere. During that time, all of the churches were starting to cater to the youth ministries, so I found myself preaching all over.

Eventually, I was asked to pastor my own church. The first church that I pastored was St. Luke Baptist Church in Halls, Tennessee. I stayed there for a short period, and that led to other opportunities to pastor other churches.

Give 'Em What They Want
Although I was young, traveling, preaching, and pastoring, nothing really changed in my life. My personality was the same. I was still a little mannish boy, but I was gifted. I could sing and preach, so it kept people drawn to me and kept me in their pulpits.

Okay, well, I did get a little full of myself.

Hell, what else could people expect from a young man who can move the crowd with his charisma?

I had the gift to the whoop, to mesmerize. I knew all of the pulpit theatrics. I learned how to make you emotional, make you shout. I was a performer. Because I had been around the older preachers that were theatrical and pulpit performers, I mimicked many of them. I took things from Jasper Williams, C.F. Franklin, and other pastors from that area. I compiled a piece of their styles, added my style, and created the perfect gimmick for myself. My gimmicks were just as good, if not better than theirs, so it kept me in somebody's pulpit. And yes, I'm admitting that a lot of pastors use gimmicks.

Okay, let me cut to the chase. When I say the phrase, Bullshit from the Pulpit, I mean just that. A lot of what you've witnessed over the years, whether in your own church, a visiting church, or on television, is a gimmick. A lot of what you see on Sunday mornings inside the pulpit is all bullshit. It's all practiced gimmicks. Preachers practice their sermons. I said what I said. And you know who you are. You practice your whoop. You practice your hallow. You practice your song; you know what your plan is. You've laid out your plan as to who you want to get to shout, who you wish to emotionalize, and how you're going to do it. And I had all of that laid out.

What separated me from the other young preachers was that I got my gimmicks from the older pastors. I wanted to be different, so I detached myself from the young preachers. I wouldn't sit down and talk to the young preachers because we were in the same boat, but I made sure to surround myself with the old guys. They had the keys to unlock the next level. So that's where I went. I'd sit up under them and soak up all their knowledge. One particular older pastor would have a group of young guys at his house and teach us how to preach. Every Saturday, we'd pile up in his home and eat the fried fish and French fries his wife would cook for us. He was a genius. He would give us all a sermon and expected each of us to master that sermon. And I would master mine. When I would get up on Sunday morning, or Sunday afternoon, I was in rare form because I knew I had the gift, and I had to use it. I can sing, so that separated me from the other preachers, and I used it to my full advantage.

If you can preach and sing, you're always one step ahead of the guy who can't hold a tune. If you can sing well, you ain't gotta preach hard. If you can make them happy, shout or fall out over a song, then all you have to do is holler. I started preaching when the message wasn't what kept people in the pews. It was all about the tune. It was the holler. My mentor taught me the art of getting people to be moved emotionally so you can do the bare minimum. Then you throw in the gimmicks to bring it all full circle. Whether it was the humming, the holler, grabbing hold of your ear and tugging, or throwing your handkerchief in the air with one hand and catching it with the other hand, being able to spin around and hearing all the women saying, "Yes! Can't he preach!"

That did it for me! I told myself that I could get used to this preaching thing. I quickly learned that the older women in the church wanted some of this young preacher, and I didn't hesitate to give them any piece of me that they wanted. Hell, I was screwing 'em all. I had them coming after me left and right. The mothers, missionaries, choir members. They'd get me by saying, "Baby, you sho' can preach." Then they'd lie and say, "You know I ain't never did this before." I would laugh, knowing damn well this ain't her first time seducing a young preacher. But I'd play along and say, "That's okay; if that's good for you, it's alright with me, just do it right now!"

Tired of This S***

After years of witnessing church folk showing their asses in and out of the pulpit, I quit preaching. I saw in the church a level of phoniness that I couldn't stomach anymore. The pastors were great bullshitters. They're great manipulators of the people. The church and the people in the church led phony lives. They pretended to be so heavenly, but yet did no earthly good, and it started to get to me. There were more fighting and backbiting behind the scenes that I'd forget where I was most times. I discovered that more evil is in the church than in the streets. People will cut your throat and throw it at your dying body in the church. People will lie on you and the church.

There were many reasons why I left the church altogether, but there was one particular incident that happened while I was a member of Ebenezer that made me go. I said something that pissed one of the head pastors one Sunday morning. He cussed me out without cussing in his sermon the following Sunday morning. And my response was, "Fuck you!"

Out of all of the lying, cheating, scandal, and evil I witnessed inside the walls of that church, it was how a nonmember of our church sealed the deal. A young homeless man by the name of Johnny, who is probably good and dead now, opened my eyes to see how so-called Christians really can be towards others. Johnny was a homeless man and in the wintertime.

The church I attended at the time was in an area called Belle Walker. Plenty of people patronized this area, including Johnny. Well, during the winter months, Johnny would try to stay warm as best he knew – and that's by sleeping in a jail cell. So, to get out of the cold and sleep in a warm place, Johnny would stand by Ulster and pull the alarm so the fire department would come and arrest him.

On many occasions, Johnny was put out of the church. He obviously wouldn't dress like the rest of them, and he always reeked of alcohol. Rather than try to help Johnny, the pastor would have him thrown out. As if on cue, when Johnny would walk through the church, they would grab him and physically throw him out of the church. By the way, Johnny was a little fellow, all of one hundred and twenty-five pounds.

Well, one Sunday morning, I was assigned to do the review on Sunday school lesson – it was about the Prodigal Son. And as I was up doing the review, I immediately thought about Johnny. I thought about his story, his journey, the way he was treated when he came into that sanctuary. I begin to compare Johnny to The Prodigal Son. At that moment, I realized that we failed Johnny. We didn't receive him with open arms, clean him up, and help him get back on the right path. Instead, we humiliated and ostracized him. I couldn't hold my tongue anymore. I asked a question to the congregation, "How is it that we as church folk can throw Johnny out of church? This is God's house. Who gives us the authority to throw Johnny out of the church?"

The pastor wasn't there, but the members of the staff told the pastor what I said. So he made a sermon, and while I was sitting in the choir stand, I listened as he talked about me. He never said my name, but I knew he was talking about me. My aunt knew he was talking about me. So I stood up, said fuck this, walked out, and never returned to Ebenezer.

After I got over what happened at Ebenezer, I found myself at Columbus Baptist Church. I went to that church for a while. I knew a few people there, so that was how I ended up there. Well, I didn't stay there for too long either. I found myself moving around from church to church for a while before I finally stopped to reflect. No matter how many congregations I joined and fellowshipped with, I still felt something was lacking from the leaders. One day, the truth hit me, and I realized that most of the pastors preached nothing but utter bullshit. Becoming aware of other books outside of the King James Version of the Bible, I began to learn some things. And that is when I walked away from the church.

Leaving church wasn't that hard for me to do because I knew that most of them were full of shit. So when I decided to stop attending church altogether, I focused on my relationship with God. I started reading, researching, and finding out different things about religion and spirituality that I didn't know. I had so many questions that no one at the church answered. So in my mind, I didn't see the point in going.

I saw people that weren't being informed, and that didn't sit right with me. Pastors and church leaders were still using that same Sunday-school book from 63 years ago to teach people about God. They were still scaring people into accepting Christ. All they preached was brimstone and fire, and that Jesus came for you to die and go to heaven. While I was still passionate about the message, it didn't move me anymore. It just became boring because it didn't deal with the real. Their messages didn't deal with people who were gangsters, who were hungry. They didn't deal with the people who didn't grow up in the church. So, where was their hope? Where was their salvation? What does God do for these people?

So I walked away.

One of my ex-wives was the sister of a very popular soul singer of the 70s. So, I was with his ministry for a while, but after going from church to church to church, I said, "Shit! Fuck this! I know who God is. My relationship with God is personal. I ain't got to deal with the bullshit from the pulpit."

What Mama Says Goes

It'll be years that I'd be away from the church until my mother kept nagging me about going back. She wore the shit out of me! "Boy, you been in church all your life. You need to go back to church. You need to go back to working for the Lord."

So I said, okay.

Now, while my mother was telling me this, I just let that marinate. Actually, it was more so her confirming what God had been telling me. The radio show that I had at the time wasn't geared towards spirituality. People knew me for being the most controversial man in town. People knew me for putting politicians on blast with all their bullshit they're up to. At some point, some of my shows begin to take on a spiritual tone. I was trying to avoid going down that path, but it kept on happening.

Then my mother got sick.

I remember my mother being in hospice. She was very sick, and I remember I went to the house. The little white nurse was there, and she said, "Your mom would not make it through the day." I remember hearing those words and letting them sink in. My mama wasn't going to make it through the day. With tears running down my cheeks, I went outside, and I asked God to give her a little more time.

My mom was a great singer. Well, my mama had come out of whatever state she was in. I don't know if it was a coma, the deadly disease, or whatever you go through before you're supposed to do whatever happens when you take your last breath. Maybe she was at the gate on the road. I don't know. I do know that she woke up singing the song, Shine On Me.

My mama lived close to a year after that.

Unspoken Love
I knew my mother was in good spirits if she was cussing. If I walked inside the house and she says, "Black motherfucker, where you been? You just getting your motherfucking ass here?" And I'd say

back to her, "It took me all motherfucking day to get my motherfucking ass here because I got a job." That's how I'd know she was in good spirits.

Most people couldn't get away with talking to their mother like that. Not even as a joke! However, that wasn't the nature of our relationship. It was more like a brother-sister bond rather than a mother-son. And for me, that wasn't a bad thing because, honestly, I was raised to connect with her as my mother. I mean, I knew who she was, but I also knew that my grandmother, and then later my aunt, were the mother-figures in my life – and that was fine with me.

In all of my life, I've never heard my mom say that she loved me. And it's not that she didn't show it. She just didn't verbally express it to me. Why? I don't know. Did it matter? Honestly, I don't know. I was so focused on my aunt's attention that I didn't feel like my mother's attention was lacking. I didn't feel any way about not having a maternal connection with my mom.

I was used to my mom not showing me verbal affection, so it didn't cross my mind that she ever would. Me being able to joke around with her was a form of her saying she loved me. So when I audibly hear my mother tell me she loves me, I'm shocked.

There was nothing special about this day, so I'm not sure what triggered mama to speak those words to me. Being our usual opinionated selves, we were just talking, and my mom says, "I love you."

Since I have never heard my mother tell me that, I had to ask her, "What you say?" I wanted her to repeat herself, so I said, "Say it again." And she did. She said, "I love you, and I always have."

That moment did something to me. Even in this moment as I rethink that moment.

I'm Not Running Anymore

Finally, the day came to lay my mother to rest. I'm pretty sure my mother was happy that I got to preach at her funeral. I had to come out of retirement for that. Nobody will be able to do it to my satisfaction. That triggered me to think about when I used to preach. I started to hear my mother's voice telling me that I need to do the Lord's work. And she was right.

So and I made a deal with God. I said, "Okay, this is the deal. If I can preach at my mother's funeral and not break down, I will stop running." I didn't break down at all. In all honesty, it was one of my finest hours.

I borrowed a friend of mine's church because my mom's church wasn't large enough for all her friends, let alone mine. Teresa Farrell and I are sitting in the limo, and it's like I said. "Remember what you said, so don't try to ignore God." Those are the words I heard as I was on my way to the cemetery. I shook my head as I see my mother's face as she scolds me about preaching again.

Since I made a vow with God, I started doing the necessary work to establish my new church.

3
The Voice of Memphis

W hen most people think of Radio Personalities, they think of the most memorable hosts. They think about the funniest, wildest, most shocking stories – and because that's what I've always done, that would define me. My audience was never disappointed when I was on the air. They knew I had information that left people squirming in their seats, hoping that I don't say their name. And I did. Every chance that I got to share what was really going down with these fools, I took it. I quickly became the Voice of Memphis for those reasons. The topics I discussed and the guests I had were definitely memorable. Just being in that environment shifted my perspective, which gave me the courage to be free with the topics and guests.

I started out working as just a deejay. I begin to form friendships and partnerships with the gospel artists and their labels, and eventually, I was asked to host different events. Since I was around different artists, I saw and heard a lot. Some of your favorite gospel singers have the nastiest attitudes, say some of the most disrespectful things, hell, most of them cuss more than I do! Many times I've seen the great names show their asses. I'd be so honored to meet some of them because, you know, I was a fan. Then I'd cross paths with them and realize they ain't shit either. They have that holier-than-thou arrogant persona, and all the while, they are heathens too.

One time I remember one of the great gospel singers showing her ass behind the scenes at a concert because they didn't have all of her money when she arrived at the venue. Oh, I'm telling you, this self-proclaimed sanctified woman used every cuss word in the book. She said, "I ain't going on that stage until I have all my motherfucking money." And she didn't. She waited until they had all her motherfucking money before she went on stage and sang about how good God is.

Then, I had a crazy ass experience with another gospel queen artist, and that shit took me by surprise. After her show, she invited me back to her room. You know, I love fucking, so I wasn't about to pass that opportunity up. When I got to the room, I notice her sissy assistant is still there. The next thing I know, they both got naked! I said, "Oh fuck this shit!" got my shit and left.

Now, I may have worked for a gospel station, but there was nothing holy or sanctified about what went down in and around that station.

Working around gospel artists showed me that most of them are not happy. For the average gospel singer, singing gospel is just a job. They really wanted to sing R&B or Blues, but they didn't have what it takes, so they settled for gospel.

I've had several radio stations with some memorable moments, but my experience back in 1992 about a woman who was fucking a dog takes the cake. I was on Mount Moriah, and this woman contacted me and wanted to come on the air to talk about her experience with this dog. She was screwing a red afghan dog. She spoke about how she met the dog and how it ended up penetrating her. My audience couldn't believe what they were hearing. Before I could get off the air, the parking lot was filled with people lined up at the radio station to see that woman who was fucking a dog. Hell, I couldn't believe she was crazy enough to admit it, but she did.

After this interview, I realized how I would get my voice heard. I couldn't do topics talking about flowers and killing roaches. I had to talk about controversial issues, like women fucking dogs.

Doing interviews like that is how my voice was amplified. I wasn't afraid to have those topics that made people uncomfortable. And in my tenure, I welcomed the chance to expose those in leadership roles for doing wrong. I didn't, and still don't mind exposing crooked pastors and dirty politicians. Now, I know some people feel that I shouldn't shed light on other pastors doing dirty deeds as a pastor myself, especially since I'm no angel. Well, the reason I don't mind exposing other pastors is that I am not a hypocrite, but they are until pastors stop pretending as if they are perfect and without sin, I'll continue to expose their dirty deeds.

One of the first Christian leaders I exposed was a guy named Dr. Frank A. Ray. He was known for screwing the female members in his church. I revealed how he had a whole apartment in the church where he entertained the females in his congregation. He had an entire hoe operation in full effect, right where people came to worship and hear a word from God. I also exposed Pastor Bobby Brooks. At the time, he was sleeping with a young girl at his church. He ended up marrying that young girl's mama.

Unfortunately, that would be one of many stories that I'd uncover about the Brooks brothers. One of the biggest stories I discovered about the Brooks brothers preachers is organizing and facilitating the first female impersonation show in Memphis. So, you have a group of pastors who openly condemn homosexuality and effeminate men yet created an atmosphere to recruit drag queens. From that one club, many others popped up. So on Saturday nights and Sunday evenings, these Christian men involved themselves in a lifestyle that they crucified their members for participating in – make it make sense.

Now, my issue is not that these men want to operate this type of business. Hey! Do what makes you happy. However, to stand in your pulpit week after week to remind people they're going to hell for leading a particular lifestyle, only to operate a business for that lifestyle is just wrong. My goal for exposing these types of leaders is to give them the courage to hold themselves accountable.

I didn't set out to use my voice this way. Let me be clear on that. Once the community realized that I had a platform and didn't mind sharing controversy on my shows, the information would just come to me. What would happen is women would be sleeping with their pastor—agreeing to be his little plaything, his toy. And when the pastor doesn't want to play with them anymore, when he wants a new toy, the women would tell on him, so to speak. They'd reach out to me and say, "Oh, the pastor is fucking so and so." And they would have proof, so I'd tell the story. They would take pictures of these men in compromising positions, keep letters and text messages to blackmail them. They'd say to me that they would say, "I'm going to Thaddeus Matthews that we fucking if you don't buy me this, that, or the other."

There was this lady who I'll never forget. I have a catalog from a woman from Jackson, Tennessee, who appeared on my show in 2019 that she put together everything that happened in that relationship. She was screwing this married preacher here in Memphis and had a whole catalog filled with every form of communication they exchanged. She had pictures of text messages that she'd blown up from him. She documented how many times he said he'd eaten her pussy, word-for-word, she got everything. Apparently, he ate her pussy so good that she decided she wanted him to eat it every day — but he's married.

So since she wanted this married man to eat her pussy every day, she decided it would be best to let his wife know. Now, the wife ain't going nowhere, and the side chick knows this, which is why she wanted to come on my show.

I remember she reached out to me about her situation. One day she called me and expresses that she wants to talk about it and expose him on the show. That's right up my alley, so I said, "Come on, baby!" So, I got her booked, and she shows up with a catalog in hand. We proceed with the show, and then suddenly, the wife texts me on my cell phone. She tells me that the side chick is not supposed to be in Memphis because they filled a restraining order and pulled up her warrant. She's broken the order so many times that she now has a warrant for her arrest. The wife texts, "Ask her!" So, I asked her about it, and she says, "Oh yeah. I did this, this and that on this date…" That's when I knew this woman was a damn fool. I said to her, "Uh, don't you think you might need to go now? She is going to send somebody over here with to whoop your ass!"

Well, this woman was unbothered because she sat there, and about 10-15 minutes later, there's a series of loud knocks on the door. I look at her. She looks at me. I'm thinking, oh hell! When the door opens, I let out a sigh of relief. I thought I would have to stop this woman from getting her ass whooped, but it was the Sheriff's Department. They came in and handcuffed her, and that was the last I heard of her.

Owning My Voice

It wasn't a hard decision for me to be a Shock, Jock. It's in my nature to be inquisitive. I don't mind asking the questions that make others choke. I don't mind surrounding myself with people who are vocal and transparent. I don't mind letting a motherfucker know what's on my mind. I don't mind owning my voice. Having said that, my voice has gotten me into some shit over the years. A few pastors have sued me. I've never lost, but they tried to stop me from using my voice this way.

As shocking as some of the content that I put out, it works for me. It's allowed me to become a household name in the Memphis area. It's opened many doors and closed some too — but opened more doors than I anticipated. Owning my voice has allowed me to move around in the community. I was able to do certain things in my community because of my name recognition. See, there aren't many areas in Memphis with a black man named Thaddeus. So, I appreciate my voice being bold and relatable.

That's all it is.

People connect with my authenticity. And the fact that I'm not afraid to cuss and spread the gospel only begets respect. Many may not like it, but they all respect it. That's my favorite part about what I do. This is why I encourage others to own their voice. When you own your voice, you can say whatever the fuck you want to say. And that's precisely what I do. That's also why I believe I'd be one of the best talk show hosts.

I'm eager to have a national stage so I can share my message with a broader audience. I think that I was born to be the best talk show host in the world. I have no problem asking you the tough questions, and that's why I'm one of the best. Everybody in this town knows who I am, whether they like me or not. They know I am the guy to get the truth to the people. Many hate me for that, but I'm okay with it.

In the meantime, I'll continue to serve those in my community.

4

Thaddy Bear

It's no secret I've been in a marriage or two… or three… or seven… I mean, who's counting? My role as a radio host contributed to the breakdown in some of my relationships. The average human cannot deal with the personality that comes with what I do.

One of my names given to me by a woman I use affectionately on the radio is Thaddy Bear. I'm known as the Thaddy Bear.

Women naturally gravitate to me, but I realize that I have to be careful of who is gravitating towards me. I need to know if it's because of who I am or what I do. I need to see if they're mesmerized by my personality or me. Most times, it's my personality.

At this point, I feel like fuck it. You either take me or leave me. The choice is yours. I'm 63 years old. Trying to separate who I am and be two separate individuals won't cut it for me. I am who I am no matter where I am or who I'm with or around. I don't put on a show. I'm not the Entertainer. If what I say and who I am is entertaining, then that's on the person. I'm not on the stage to be an Entertainer, to make you laugh. If you laugh, you laugh.

My gift is my mouth, and that's what I do. That's who I am.

Thaddy Bear is the side of me that gets the ladies. I don't know if it's a combination of my personality and my manhood or not, but I have no problem getting women. Never have. Hell, I was married fifty-leven times! But I couldn't stay married because, well, I couldn't stop fucking other women.

I used to believe that I was actually addicted to sex. I started at a young age and have been getting it ever since. I was around 15 or 16 years old the first time I had oral sex. When I was in high school, I got turned out by the bus driver. I'll never forget that lady. She was a demon! Yep, she was a sex demon straight from the pits of hell. She taught me so many different nasty things on the back of the school bus.

It was my last year of school. I had to take the bus to Fraser High School, and she was the bus driver. She taught me the fine art of oral sex. We did all kinds of ol' nasty shit. We fucked every single time I rode that bus. She showed me everything I needed to know about fucking. She helped me perfect my stroke. She showed me how to speed it up, slow it down, and do it from the back, from the side, upside-down, inside-out. She taught me all that shit!

It got to the point that I would go to her house.

Now, I'm about 17, 18 years old. I was hooked. She was like my drug dealer. She gave me my first hit, and I was instantly hooked.

While I was pussy whipped for sure, I was clear that it wasn't love. It was all about the fucking. It was not about emotions. It definitely was not about feelings. So, when it was time for us to go our separate ways, it didn't bother me at all. Shit, I was grateful! That woman taught me how to fuck, and to this day, I never disappoint.

Because of my affectionate nickname and persona, I stayed in trouble. Being on the radio brought me so many opportunities it was hard for me to pass them all up. When I went to the radio, I was like a star to those women. They treated me like royalty, and I let 'em. Every one of 'em. These women threw themselves at me. They'd tell me about the shows they listened to, how hearing my voice made them feel, and it just broke me! No matter how many women I've been with, I'd still be so fascinated with women. Hell, they were just as fascinated as I was.

Fucking became an addiction for me. I had to have sex almost daily. And I didn't care what woman I'd have it with. I had all kinds of women giving me pussy. I didn't want none of 'em. It was just a sex thing for me. So I didn't care if she was a married woman. She could get it, too.

I didn't play any games to get it, either. I was honest about what I wanted. I'd let them know; I don't pay bills. I'm just going to fuck you. I'm going to talk to you right, we are going to get freaky, have a good time, and I'm going to send you home to your husband.

Most of you read that last part and cringed or even called me out of my name, but hear me out. It's not that I don't care about women. I love them. But I also know what they do to me sexually, and I loved that part the most. To be honest, sex is why I got married so many times. Some of the women I was with had me saying, "Yeah, I'll marry you," basically just because I had to have it.

My sex addiction got so bad that I had sex with a midget. Yep, sure did. Right at the radio station. She called me and said, "you sound tall." I told her to come and see. So she showed up at the radio station. The building was downtown in an old building, but she showed up. I could see the top of her head as she walked across the street. The radio station had a lot of steps. It was like watching her climb a mountain to get to where I was at. We ended up having sex on the couch. She put all that big ol' ass up in my face, and I fucked her good. She got under my desk, sucked my dick, and I've never seen her since.

That was just one of the many sexual escapades I've had on the clock. I had it down to a science. I could put a record on. I screwed while the record was on. If the song were three minutes long, then I'd know that I have two and a half minutes to get it.

I'd get women to come to the radio station, and while the records were on, we would get down on the floor and screw. Then I would get up and pray to the Lord!

Yeah, that was my life. That was the persona that I had in those early days of radio. Now that I'm older, I'm at a different point in my life.

Single Again

People who don't know my life would assume my marriages didn't work because I was cheating, and they're right. But! There were other reasons. Reasons like the fact that I don't take no shit!

In all seriousness, I grew tired. I was not faithful to any of my wives. Do I regret divorcing any of them? Not really. Well, there's only been one wife that I wish I had made things work, and that's my youngest daughter's mom. The demise of that relationship shifted my perspective a little. And it was my fault. I was being good ol' Thaddy Bear. I was cheating. Then she started cheating after she found out that I was cheating. Well, her cheating was a little different since the man she was screwing was a friend of mine.

I remember the first time that I got an inkling of what was going on. It was on a Sunday afternoon. I remember it so well because at the time, on Sunday nights, I emceed the gospel shows in Dawson. This particular incident, we're living in these apartments in the Whitehaven area of the city. She was going to be at the very same program that night. Sundays were always busy for me, and that day was no different. I came home because I had to change clothes for the event and was surprised to see her there, still getting dressed. She was supposed to be heading to the event.

My little girl was getting dressed also, so I asked her when she was leaving and how she was getting there. She said her cousin was going to pick her up. I didn't think anything of it. So this car comes to the apartment to pick her up. I picked up the baby and said, "I'm going to go outside with you, take my baby to the car." As I was taking the baby out the door of the apartment, she stops me.

She used the excuse not to go out in the rain because I had to speak that night. So she goes on, but she had to come back to the house because she forgot something. This time I go out with her. I look at the car. That wasn't her cousin's car. But I didn't stop her. It didn't take long for someone else to spot her in another man's car and tell me.

When I realized that she's fucking someone I know, I flip. I didn't give a fuck that we were at church when I found out.

It didn't help that when I started doing the calculations, she came to the door with him holding my baby. My eyes were glued to them as he walks in and sits on the second row. I immediately got up and went to my car. I got my gun out of the car. After that, I went blank. I don't even think I came back in the same way that I went out. I'm enraged now, and it wasn't so much about her. He was holding my baby.

I came back around to where he was seated, and I pulled my gun out. I place it at the back of his head. Ready to pull that trigger. Slap! I turn around, and I'm face to face with a friend of mine. She hit my hand and said, "She ain't worth it." It was like the light came on. I scanned the room, shook my head, and said, "Man, you know you're right." I took the gun, put it in my car, and left.

Life After Marriage

Marriage is a beautiful thing but a hideous thing with the wrong person. I know I've had my share of unions, but if I had to give a tip to somebody, it would be 'don't do it until you know you're ready to do it.' How do I feel about marriage now? It's essential, and I'm sure I'll get married again. I mean, I don't want to die in my house by myself. Die alone, and now I'm stinking and stuff. Nope, it won't be me. I'm getting married again.

Nobody wants to be alone. You take a different perspective of loneliness and being alone at an old age. It will take a particular type of woman for me to marry again. She has to be open to cooking and cleaning and all that stuff, be affectionate, freaky, nasty, and all that. A woman who understands who I am and what I do and what my life mission is all about now. One that can deal with the fact that I'm going to be around women and not be insecure. They're going to be in my face, but at the end of the day, I'm coming home. I don't care about some of the things I cared about when I was a real young man. I'm trying to put some things for this world that we live in.

5

Loving Two Ain't Easy To Do

If someone had told me that I would be in love with two women at the same time, I wouldn't have believed it, mostly since that wasn't what I was trying to do. I was okay being a single man and fucking who I wanted, where I wanted, when I wanted, and where I wanted – but then these two incredible women came into my world and shook that motherfucker up!

Now, I know someone is reading this and saying, "Why didn't you just choose one?" well, that's easier said than done when you're getting what you want from both women. And I don't mean just sex. I mean companionship. Both of these women believed in me, believed in my vision, and it was hard for me to choose.

So for years, I didn't.

And I mean years!

Del had been my personal assistant for about six years. She handled my business affairs for me. Before you start judging me, understand that our relationship did not start with her having the role that she had at the time. Let me explain.

See, I met Del first. Right around the time that I separated from my wife. I was scheduled to be divorced the following year, so I started fucking again. Around the time that I started seeing Del, I was also involved with another young lady that I had recently met by the name of Melanie. Yep, their names are similar, and nope, I can't make this up!

Even though I was interested in Melanie, I didn't consider having more than just a sexual relationship with her because she was a married woman. That didn't stop me from wanting to fuck her, though. And I did every chance I got.

To be clear, in meeting Del, there was no intention of it being more than a fling. Sure, she was an intelligent woman, I liked her, but I wasn't looking to jump back into a committed relationship. I wanted to enjoy being Thaddy Bear without the headache. So I didn't think twice about fucking Del and Melanie because, well, I was a kind of a single man.

Well, it may sound like all fun and games to fuck two different women, but when the shit hits the fan, it ain't all that fun! Melanie, the married woman was in love with me, and Del was equally in love with me, so I quickly became the prime character of a song called, Trying To Love Two Ain't Easy To Do. Again, I know I should have cut it off with one of them, but I couldn't. To be honest, I was in love with both of them too, and I wanted them both, so I kept dating them both. I had Melanie and Del. That was weird as shit too! Their names were so damn close you can easily say the wrong name. I won't confirm or deny if I've fucked up a few times with the name thing. But I will say, I started calling Melanie, Tee.

Back to my love triangle.

As I stated, I didn't intend to fuck Del. It kind of just happened. The job that she had at the time was fading out. I had basically worked as a solo act in my business, and I needed help. I didn't have an assistant helping me do anything, but I desperately needed one. I was looking for bigger and better opportunities. I was ready to increase my territory and she was the one who could help me. So, I created the assistant's job, not knowing that in a very few months, hell, I would need one.

After talking to Del and telling her what I needed, she came on as my assistant. And then my lover. She had been my backbone; we had a strong friendship, great chemistry. The only thing that's fucked up about us is the nature of our relationship.

It became too difficult for her to see me in Thaddy Bear mode. To be fair, I understand. I've tried to juggle two women, along with others, for an extended time. Although Del knew that I had several women when I met her that was interested in me, she decided to deal with me anyway. And to be fair, I don't think that she expected to grow the types of feelings she had for me either. But hey, I'm just that kind of fella.

We call it that Matthews Magic. Yes, we.

Believe it or not, I used to have women falling at my feet. But there were only two women that could hold my interest, that was Tee and Del. And even though I had other women and even though she knew later on up the road about Del, I'm mean about Tee, see, there I go. It was not until something very personal in the relationship happened that changed Del's mentality.

What The Fuck Is Post-Partum?
If there's ever a definition of driving somebody crazy, then it would be based on where Del was with me before we parted ways. Her ass turned into a crazy woman that I didn't recognize anymore. Well, at least that's what I thought when I noticed her ass acting a damn fool.

After all of the bumping and grinding Del and I were doing, she eventually became pregnant. It would have been a little boy.

Yes, would have been.

We were going to name him Thaddeus Matthews II because I hate that word junior. So yeah, unfortunately, Del lost the baby. She found out that she was carrying him in her tubes.

The day I found out she was pregnant, she was about four months pregnant. She went to a doctor, and the doctor told her that the baby was in her tubes and that she would not be able to deliver a child. So, she had the operation that women have in that type of situation. I don't know whether you would call it a miscarriage or... it's not an abortion, but she was not able to deliver the child.

And after finally understanding what happens to a woman when she conceives a child, I now understand that's what drove her crazy, not me.

Okay, can we have an honest moment? This is one reason why this chapter is so important to me because I want men to understand a woman's emotions. There's so much that men don't know about the chemistry or the hormonal imbalance that takes place during pregnancy. That beautiful experience can breed some ugly reactions within women, and it's almost like they can't control it. Learning why Del was so emotional about the loss of her baby really helped me forgive some things that transpired after that experience.

I was asked how did I feel about her being pregnant. Well, I think when she told me, she said to me that the baby was in her tubes and that the baby was going to have to be, not done away with, but she was going to have the operation. I didn't know what I felt. I said, "Okay, well, you've got to do what you got to do. I know that it can endanger your life." So, my feelings were, even though I was involved with Melanie, there is a love and a bond that I have for Del that will take me to my grave. I don't know, as a man, I didn't know what to feel. It's a baby that I had no real emotional attachment to. My attachment was to the woman, not the child that I did not know. And I think that happens with many men because we don't understand the attachment women have with the baby. So, I don't know how I felt because I had no bond, had no attachment with the child that I did not know.

After the dust settled with the loss of the baby, my relationship with Del drastically changed. Del went crazy. She lost her damn mind. I just thought the motherfucker was crazy. One day

I said to her, bitch are you crazy? Because her whole psyche changed!

She became someone that I didn't understand—the words manic depression was brought up. When I learned about that, I understood what she was experiencing. Then, I found out about the thing that women go through after having or losing a baby, postpartum depression. Del was dealing with this, which caused her to gather an attachment to me that was not normal.

She became overly obsessed, overly protective. We never argued before the pregnancy. We didn't argue about anything. We didn't argue about the women or anything else. All of a sudden, we were at each other's throats for stupid shit. It was as though a rage built up in her. It made it hard to deal with her on a personal level.

Now, as far as my business, she was dead on it. At the time, I didn't know how I would function without her business-wise, but it became a burden on the relationship. Things got real, and I had to decide how I wanted to deal with Del going forward. She got arrested one night. We had a disagreement at her house, and shit got real. I don't even remember what the fuss was, but she went into a rage that I had never seen. And I'm an old guy in the street, so I've had plenty of women, and I'm telling you, I had never seen that type of rage.

Things got so heated between us that I began to literally run from this woman. As I was trying to get away from her, I ran outside of her house. Do you know this woman followed me outside? She's butt ass naked, following me out, acting an ass. So here our grown asses are, battling in front of her house. She's outside the house, naked, and I'm saying, "Del go back in the house. You are naked." I didn't want to see her like that. Deep down, I felt terrible. But I was also worried about this shit getting out to the public.

Here I am, one of the most known personalities in this town, standing outside with a naked woman cussing my ass out. If the police show up at this house, it will be all over the news, and it's gonna be my fault. No matter if people know that I'm actually the innocent one here, it's still going to be my fault. I didn't have time for that shit!

So, I jumped in my car to get away from this scene. Del's holding on to my door. She eventually falls, but I didn't know she fell, let alone held onto the door, so I kept going. I didn't look back either. All I know was that I got away from her.

Or so I thought.

Next thing I know, I'm getting a call from her. I answer, and she asks, "Where are you at?" I'm not fooling with Del, so I try to brush her off. Well, that wasn't a good idea because she puts on her clothes, grabs her gun, and goes to Prive. She knows that's one of my hangouts, so she took it upon herself to come see me about a thing or two. I was told that she was to the front door of the club with her gun. I get wind that she's at Prive showing her ass, so I called her phone.

The security people answer the phone. They found her trying to get in with her gun, so they put her under arrest. I shook my head. This is exactly the type of shit I was trying to avoid but somehow still found myself in. I pulled up to the club, and there she is, sitting on the curb in handcuffs. They won't let me approach her, so I just stand back and watch as they take her to jail. As wrong as she was in that moment, I couldn't let her go to jail, especially since I'm the reason she was out there acting a damn fool. Since I've got the right connections in the city, I made sure her charges were dropped before she even made it to the precinct. I don't think she even got back to where the rest of the prisoners were. I made the calls, and she was released the next morning in court. I got a lawyer; it was all squashed and did away with.

Unfortunately, that wasn't the only time that I had to get a case thrown out for Del acting psychotic. The other time was because she and Melanie had gotten into it. We were used to Del acting crazy, but this time Melanie was over the drama.

We've had several incidents where Del would pop up in my house unexpected, unannounced, uninvited, and just banging on my damn doors—texting me all hours of the day and night. And you know, women have this thing when they get mad at another woman, and then everybody's a bitch. Del would say something like 'This bitch over here, Melanie, fuck that bitch over there.' Del would just pop up at my house, banging on the damn door because she saw Tee's car in my house, or somebody would pass by my house and call Del and say, "You know, that car over there at his house." Then she would jump up because she didn't live far from me; she'd jump up and would bang on my door until I opened up. I said, damn, this crazy bitch. Then I got to go through essays on the damn text. How I'm a no-good motherfucker. Low life motherfucker. If you want that bitch Baba, Baba, Baba, Baba. Bitch this, bitch that. God damn!

One day I said to myself, okay. I hear Baba, Baba, from Melanie and Baba, Baba from Del. I'm hearing the bitch this, bitch that, bitch that from both of them. I'm caught up in between two women and don't know what to do. I know you're probably wondering when or if I learned my lesson or not.

This is the part of the message for men: leave that shit alone.

Dealing with two women gets nerve-wracking, plus dangerous. Del had a goddamn Glock on her hip, and this crazy motherfucker hits 98 every time she goes to the goddamn range. This big Amazonian woman is able when I'm in public to keep folk off of me. It's just crazy shit. Crazy. I chose the wrong type of woman to dabble in and out with. Over the years, I've fucked women all over the goddamn country, and I never ran into this type of shit before. Melanie, Del, name sounds just alike. Shit, I need a drink every time I have the damn discussion.

Melanie filing a restraining order was because she was over the back and forth. They were supposed to go to court, but I got that squashed. I didn't want them to have a criminal record over this mess.

The altercation that pushed Melanie over the hedge happened during the birthday party I was having at the church. So, I'm standing there, entertaining guests, then I look out my peripheral, and I see Del making a stride. She's walking like Oprah Winfrey in the scene in The Color Purple. You know when she's going to cuss Miss Celie out for telling Harpo to beat her. Yep, she looked just like that! Melanie was on the other side of the gym, and that's where Del was headed. All I could think is that I hope this woman doesn't act up in this church. I couldn't have them getting into it over me at my 62nd birthday party. My next thought is, I got to get them apart. They didn't get physical, but they got loud, loud enough to cause a small disruption. My security people, members of the church and her family all came rushing to the back to see what the commotion was all about.

I guess Melanie was done dealing with Del's bullshit, so she decided to go and file a restraining order, and Del gets served.

All I could do was shake my head because yet again, here I am, trying to sort out some shit that shouldn't be a problem. But because Del couldn't keep her emotions in check, here we are.
Now, this was a big deal in our town. Everyone heard about what happened and knew that Tracey was the reason Del had to go to court. And of

course, everyone's expecting me to show up at the court date because it's going to be a real circus now, it's going to be entertainment, and that's the reason I didn't want Tee to go through with it.

Del goes to court. Tee has gotten dressed to go to court. Tee is at work. I call Tee on her job, and I tell her, don't go because it will put me in an embarrassing situation. I reminded her of who the media would be out for. They'd be out for me. Eventually, I get Tee not to show up that morning, which was not easy to do. That particular morning, she was all gung-ho about pressing charges. She was mad at Del and even left the church. Del was still going crazy. I was just in the middle of two crazy ass women!

What Men Should Know About Postpartum
In the mindset of a man that does not understand postpartum depression, it is craziness. As men don't understand sometimes, the anger or the rage that a woman has is brought on because of the impregnation of a woman. And see, you think that a man, me... would think that having the baby gives you the bond, holding the bond, holding the child in your arms, sucking your titty and all that, that gives you the bone. But I found out through this particular experience that the bond is in the womb, the nine months of the carrying of the child, in her case only four months. But that is a psychological

thing that happens with a mother and a child that a man does not understand. Had Del not gotten pregnant, this wouldn't be an issue. She wouldn't give a fuck one way or the other about what I was doing. She wouldn't give a fuck about Melanie, Sueann, Bromquisha, none of that. But there is an attachment that Del has to me that is solely based on the fact that she was pregnant with my child and lost it.

The advice that I give to a man experiencing this is, first of all, to gain the knowledge of what pregnancy and bonding are all about. That's the first thing. And understand that the woman cannot love the child that she gives birth to or carries unless she loves you. And the love that Del has for me is not sexual. It ain't based on the sex at all. It's based on the fact that I was the father of her child that she'd never have, she'll never see.

I believe because we've had conversations, just riding along, what our son would've been doing. That he would've been called The Cussing Baby, he would've been sitting on the front row at church. When I'd be preaching, he'd be sharply dressed like his daddy. So, I would hear these conversations, and I'm just saying, okay, you know, she's just talking about the what-ifs of life. But really, that was a psychological bond, that was a release, that was a purging, that was the releasing of a hurt. In her mind, she could see that boy sitting on the front row of the church, that boy saying, I want to be like my dad. My name is Thaddeus, too. So, my advice is to understand the woman and understand that if you're going through that right now, the rage and you got a crazy ass woman, the craziness was brought on by the fact that you impregnated her. And especially if that child is a child that is not here, not a woman who has gone to get an abortion but a woman that wanted the baby, was ready for the baby, had a name for the baby, had dreams, goals, and aspirations for the baby and then she loses that. It's like I talked about from the pulpit. It's the grief factor, and what Del has had to deal with, is grief. And all suffering is not physical death, but in this case, there is physical death, even though she did not know the child, had never seen the child, that was a physical death that took place. And some of the anger comes from the fact that I don't feel the same grief.

Can't Have My Cake

I've never been the type to give a fuck about what people think of me. However, I want people to know reading this book or hearing me in the media because although I'm a pastor and spiritual leader, I'm fucked up sometimes, too. We all are. I'm transparent, and I'm okay with telling my truth. I fully understand that we all have sinned and come short of the glory of God. We are all being made and molded by God, and that no matter who we are, God reaches down and picks us up.

One of my many downfalls is my flesh. I love women. I love fucking women. I love fucking women that are smart, intelligent, and attractive – all the things that Del was. People have asked me why I didn't just pick her since she meant so much to me. Well, over the years of being Del's lover and friend, I learned that we are better off as friends. She's a very dominant one. She's a very aggressive woman. She's been known to beat up the mother hoes, and I don't stand for that shit. And I mean, that's where it is, at this point. At this point, Del and I have come basically to the conclusion, since some things happen, that the relationship, the personal connection, the intimate relationship, the fucking has to be over. We realized that we should go forth as friends and business partners, building a media empire, whatever that happens, building a ministry, whenever it happens. And I have to understand that there are going to be other men in her life. They'll never measure up to me. They'll never come close to me. They will always be in my shadow. That will be a fear of some of them because they cannot meet up to who I am, and they're correct. They are correct. But she has to be able to deal with the fact of me with someone else, as well.

I know better than anybody else, Del believed in who I am, or else she wouldn't have been a part of my businesses. As they say, all good things have to come to an end, and things ended romantically between her and me. And that was for the best. She does so much. She's so creative and contributed to my vision in such a huge way. And I guess that was one reason I have the love and attachment that I have for her because she is such an asset to who I am in all of these capacities. But I also knew that I had to let her go.

So I did.

6

The One for Thaddy

It's no secret that I've been married quite a few times, and for that reason, I wasn't in a rush to marry again. I knew that I'd do it again eventually because, hey, I'm not the type of man to be alone. I just want to make sure I get it right before I get married again.

And I think I finally got it right with Melanie.

I wasn't looking for Mel. I was just enjoying myself out one night, and she caught my attention and held it ever since.

I met Melanie in 2015 at a little hole in the wall Blues club. It was a Sunday evening, and I was just sitting back, enjoying the scenery. We live in a small town, but I hadn't seen her before. It was hard not to notice her. She was strutting across the club in a pair of tight-fitting jeans that made her ass look good. She had on a pair of ten-inch heels that made her even sexier than she already appeared to be. And I'm an ass person, so I looked at her and thought, this woman is fine.

At first, I told myself not to bother her. Told myself I would be good that night, that I ain't gonna mess with anybody. But she came walking in my direction, and I couldn't help myself. So, I finally introduce myself to her. She wasn't excited and enthused too. So, I had to bring out that Thaddeus Matthews magic. After I told her who I was, I can tell that she liked me a little bit. We drank some drinks. And we sat down and talked. And at the end of the night, I got her number, and we went from there.

Now, I didn't know what to expect from dealing with her. She had a little husband, but that didn't stop me from being interested in her. We started to see each other regularly. She came to my house regularly and then would go home to the husband. And then she stopped going home. That's the Matthew's magic again.

Over time, our relationship grew. And then I got the idea. I'm going to take her from her husband. At the time, I didn't think she would leave her husband. But then... that Matthew's magic kicked in. I got divorced, and when I got divorced, she came to me, and she said, because she was spending a lot of time with me, her husband knew that she had a man. I mean, it was hard not to see because I'd give her roses and stuff. She always took the roses to the house. He'd get pissed off and get in his feelings and stuff. Hey! It wasn't my fault he couldn't contain his wife!

Not sure if she just didn't love him anymore, whatever the situation was. I think he suffered from erectile dysfunction, so she asked him if she could have a boyfriend. So, you know, I became the boyfriend. Eventually, she left her husband to be with me.

Melanie and I have been together for six years. The only complication, the only argument that we had was always about Del. That's the only thing that we've ever argued about. Other than that, I was definitely in love with her. Initially, those ten-inch heels caught my attention, but it was her conversation, her mind that kept me intrigued.

Now, before you ask me, well, why did you mess around with Del. Well, because Del is a great woman, too, I didn't want to deal with both of them at the same time, but before I knew it, I was in love with two women.

I got in so deep. I didn't want to hurt either woman. But I knew that at some point, I was going to have to make a choice – and that wasn't easy. Apparently, Del and I had gotten carried away with our bumping and grinding because she had gotten pregnant. Now, that was not something I was ready for. Not only was I not planning to have more kids, but I had Mel. And I knew she wasn't about to put up with me, Del, and a baby. As much as I didn't want to, I had to let Mel know what was going on.

So, I was kind of forced to choose Del when she got pregnant. That was one of the most challenging conversations that I had with Mel. I knew that she didn't want to hear about Del being pregnant, but I had to tell her.

I remember the day I told her—one of the hardest decisions I had to make. Choose love or my future. I must be honest. I had to think about my future. Truth is, Del had my future in the palm of her hands. She ran my business, the church, my livelihood. I couldn't diss her and be stuck. It seems like being with Del was the best option at the time.

One night, while I was sitting in a bar, Del did one of her usual pop-ups. Even though she was upset with me about everything that was happening between us, I still cared for her. I didn't want to lose Del because my feelings for her were also real. I also didn't want to destroy my ministry at the church or my business. What's a man to do?

Well, this night at the bar, when Del approached me, I took a different approach. I didn't know what state of mind she was in. I didn't want to trigger her. I thought, hell, I've already caused the woman so much pain. So, out of concern for Del, I told Melanie that I wanted to be with Del. And that did not go over well... and I mean at all.

One thing about Mel is that she's in control of her emotions. So, while she had every right to fuss, cuss, and scream at my black ass, she didn't. She did nothing most people would expect for a woman in her shoes to do. While she didn't get loud or start screaming, I can tell that I hurt her. And damn, that made me feel like shit.

For weeks, all I could think about was how Mel felt about me choosing Del. Nothing against Del at all, but in my heart of hearts, I knew that Mel was the one that I belonged with. It doesn't take away what I had with Del. It's just not meant for Del and me to be together long term. It's Mel. Mel is the yin to my yang.

I realized that after contacting her. It was clear that she felt the same way because we picked up where we left off, and I was happy about that.

Why Her?
You're probably wondering how I ended up choosing Mel. Well... I love her. And to be frankly honest, I had had enough of playing with two

women. It's too damn hard and too much damn work. So, we both decided that it was time for us to move forward. I was tired of the bullshit. So, I decided that me and Mel will be together.

Why her? She's a pretty girl; she's a smart girl. I've watched her advance in the six years that we've known each other. And she loves me too. Sure, there are days she hates me, but she loves me, and I love her back.

One of my favorite things about Melanie is that she's not a fan. She's not impressed with me being Thaddeus Matthews. She's not impressed with me being on the radio, or on TV, or with me being popular. In fact, she likes me better than The Cussing Pastor or my other monikers, the Thaddy Bear. I don't know the difference between them because it's all me. But her view on it is that my persona is different as Thaddeus, plain old dumb ass Thaddeus than it is as The Cussing Pastor. My ego does not drive her. I'm driven a lot by my ego. I'm driven a lot by who I am. I'm driven a lot by, at 63 years old, I got some things I need to accomplish before that.

Lesson to the Fellas
Now, I know most young men think it's cool to have multiple women, but I'm here to tell you that it's not all that it's cracked up to be. You could lose

your life playing around with women and their emotions. That is something I will never do as long as I live.

If you see an opportunity to fuck with two women at the same time, son, I'm telling you, don't get in there. Don't get in. Stay away from that shit. There's an old William Bill song, "Trying To Love Two Ain't Easy To Do," and that couldn't be more true. I believe that you can love more than one person. But I don't think that you love them equally. Everybody we end up in relationships with plays a significant role in our lives, on our journeys. Everybody serves a purpose. The same is true for Del and Mel. Both of these women are very protective of me. They were good to me, they were patient with me, they were influential in my life, and they took care of me. I just did some pretty fucked up shit to them both over the years.

Okay, I can admit my faults, and I, Thaddeus Matthews, was wrong from going back and forth between two women. I can admit that I did the lying and did the cheating. And I'm telling you, young men reading this, not to play that game. I know it looks enticing, but it's not.

Is it hard to resist? Absolutely but you better come up with a game-plan. One way to avoid this mistake is by saying no to the temptation. That's it. I mean, that's the only thing that you can do. It's saying no to the temptation.

That's what got me caught up, temptation. If I had that in control, I would have avoided the emotional drama that this situation brought on.

See, when I met both of these women, I did not expect to fall in love with either of them. Del was a fling. And Mel was married, so I didn't see any real commitment happening with her. But in some form, we did commit. We committed to what we had and, over time, became a couple. We went everywhere together, didn't give a damn who saw us.

It Was My Fault
It's imperative to me that people understand that I know that I wasn't shit. It's not either of the women's fault. It was all my fault. I can take being the bad guy. I can take folks buying the book just to read about this old dirty motherfucker. I can handle that. But both of these women are intricate parts of my life, and they've both been good to me. I'm the motherfucking that ain't been no damn good. This whole issue, whatever it is, was brought about by me. I'm being honest. I was trying to have my cake and eat it too. But it's important for people to know that I was the scoundrel. People know me as a scoundrel. And I'm okay with that. Just don't

throw these women under the bus. Neither of them deserves it.

7

He Said What Now?

Alright, so let's talk about how the world knows about me. Most people know me from preaching and being a shock jock in Memphis. And quite a few people found out about me because I went viral on the internet.

Now, let me just say this. I don't really know or care about going viral. That's what this new generation calls it. It wasn't something I planned to do. I was just being myself, and ya'll start sharing the video with other people. Ya'll started calling me The Cussing Pastor. And well, now we're here.

So the video that took me viral was a conversation I had on December 17, 2017. At that time, I was on Facebook Live, talking about the tragic murder of NBA basketball star Lorenzen Wright by his wife, Sherra.

I revealed a lot of information about what happened on my platform. So I had a lot of people calling me about this particular story. I'm not really sure of the circumstances, but word had come out that his mother needed some money to do something, so we raised $6,500 on-air, in checks and cash. All the checks were made out to her, and we took to his mother $6,500. The next day, which was a Saturday, I was in my office at a church, and I talked about it. I was on the air, maybe three or four hours, talking about the case and talking about a Sherra. And at the very end of this lengthy video, I went into about a three-minute cussing rant. At that particular moment, the last thing on my mind was that people would be offended that I cussed, let alone make such a big deal about it that it would be shared all across the internet for millions of people to see.

Well, that's exactly what happened. Later that day, I found out that someone had cut the cussing out and posted a snippet on Facebook. Hundreds of thousands of people had something to say to me about the video. Never mind the hours I spent talking about something important. All people saw was a man cussing. To be fair, no other context was shown or given. They didn't know anything about the other part of what I was saying, so I get it. What I didn't get was why someone would deliberately go out of their way to do it. It was designed to make me look bad as a preacher.

And in many ways, to many people, it did. But I don't give a fuck about what those motherfuckers have to say about what I'm saying or doing.

Most preachers would be spilling over, crying, and rebuking these people. Not me. I wish I could find them now and buy them a steak and a bottle of champagne. I don't know who it was, but they're probably kicking themselves in the ass and thinking, "Damn, I made him big." So if you just so happened to be reading this: thank you!

So yeah, the post went viral, as this generation says. So many people were watching, sharing, and commenting on the video. I saw, and the numbers were jumping that evening. It was over 100,000 when I saw it. That Monday, it was up to 2.3 million people. Yep, that many people had viewed it in that short time. And the numbers were continuing to rise.

I couldn't believe that many people saw that video.

Well, doing that did wonders for my platform. I was scrolling through the comments to see what people were saying. I saw one common phrase being used. They were calling me 'the cussing pastor.' I know it's not an Emmy Award-winning title, but it's so befitting. So, I tapped into my businessman mindset, took the name, cussing pastor, trademarked and copyrighted it and all that stuff, and that's how I became.

I'm Viral, Now What?

Well, nothing's really changed after going viral. I still do my daily videos, host my radio show, run my church, my businesses – I'm still the same ol' Thaddeus. At least that's how I see it.

Since my initial viral moment, I've gotten thousands of views. At this point, I expect to go viral. Not in an arrogant way. I expect that what I say is going to trigger somebody. I know for a fact I can trigger folks. I've had other moments that have gone viral and gotten some attention for doing just that. In some situations, I was stirring the pot, others I had nothing to do with their situation, just got mixed up.

For instance, social media mixed me up with Reverend Wilson. Now, let me clear this up. I am not the same man who got caught eating pussy on Facebook. I eat pussy. I just don't get caught on film doing it. Because people taught that I was him, my followers on Instagram went up when that happened.

I was at nearly 170,000 followers at that point because I went viral when I was talking about that ugly ass K. Michelle. I also went viral with singing sensation, as they said, Tank. Yes, they said that about him, not me. But yeah, we had it out.

People always ask me why I even bother. Hell, I look at it as a business. Going viral increases my viewers and the people I'm connected with. It's helped my networking abilities. That video and many other videos going viral have gotten me my first national TV appearance on Tosh 2.0. Hell, I didn't even know who Tosh was. But that video got me an airplane flight to California. And dragging the others, well, that's just for fun.

Yeah, I Said It
I hate that bitch, K. Michelle. That skinny, thinking she can sing, bitch irks me, makes my asshole itch. I had two separate altercations with that bitch. The first incident was when she got evicted here in Memphis. She was renting a mansion for $10,000 a month. Well, she got evicted from the mansion, and when the court order came for her to leave, she painted the walls pink, hot pink. She's a destructive bitch. She just went through the house, painting it pink. Well, I have a source close to the case that let me know what was really going on. When I found out, I aired her funky, dirty ass laundry. She loves to pretend like she got all this money, but in essence, she's a broke bitch. So, I put her ass on blast. You can't argue

with the documents, with the receipts, and I had all the receipts. So, she took a disliking to me. She went on social media and said some things. And I went to social media, and I had some things to say about her and her little sister-boyfriend. She got a little boyfriend that's a dentist; he's more of a bitch than her.

The second time I ran into this hoe is at a Cajun place that was an advertiser on my show. So, I went in there. I didn't even notice her. She was already sitting in there. She and her little sweetheart of a boyfriend was sitting in there, him looking like Daisy Mae. So, I went and sat at my usual spot, and I hadn't paid her any mind. She saw me first and decided that she didn't want to share the same air as me. So, she went to the management and demanded that they put me out because she was present. I thought to myself, bitch.

I gathered my thoughts and said, "Y'all go tell that raggedy looking bitch to put me out her goddamn self. She and her sweet ass boyfriend." Well, naturally, I was a good customer because I go in there two or three times a month. I spent almost $100 every time I went in there, so damn it, they weren't going to get rid of me. You just go in there now and then. She decided she wasn't going to stay, so she left. Once she got up and left, I laughed my ass off. Oh, she didn't like that. The bitch gets crazy, "I'm a whoop his ass." So, I get from my table, and I start walking towards them. They left after I cursed them out really good and called her the little cheap looking scallywag, bitch that she is.

I continued my meal and thought about what just happened. I guess it wasn't mean for me to be a part of that project. Guess that's the end of that!

Right?

Wrong.

She goes to the police department in Downtown Memphis and files a complaint on me. I get a call on my phone that K. Michelle was trying to get me arrested. I asked, "For what?" The officer replied, "You're harassing her." I said, "Look, I'm down here eating dinner." So, they said, "Thaddeus, don't worry about it. We are just telling you what it was." So, that's what happened with K Michelle and me. I pissed her off. She tried to get me arrested and failed. And yes, I still can't stand her ass.

Let's see. Oh yeah, I've gotten into it on Facebook with Judge Maybelline and Evelyn Braxton, you know, them Braxton girls mama. Now, I don't know either one of these women.

They were doing a live recording at a radio station, and then they bring up The Cussing Pastor. They talked about how I ain't saved and how I ain't going to heaven. So, you know I lit in on their ass. And in Thaddeus Matthews fashion, I went on my show and let them know exactly how I felt about them putting my name in their mouths. I talked about Judge Maybelline being a bad wig-wearing motherfucker. How the fuck are you going to talk about somebody? And I had to remind Miss Braxton to get them whore ass daughters she has in check. You know, the ones that can keep no man. They are always complaining about what's going on with them. Yeah, get them motherfuckers in check before you comment on me because I don't give a fuck about you or your thoughts about me. So, yeah, that video went viral too.

Hmm, who else? Oh yeah, Tank, the sweetheart that he is. He had something to say about a picture I posted. A lady had been in my office at the church getting married and came by the church to visit and tell me about her getting married. I think she brought an offering to the church; I don't turn an offering away. She came to the church and wanted to meet with me. So, I'm in my office, sitting behind my desk. She decided she wanted to take a picture with me. She came around my desk to take the picture, a clear vision, in my opinion. Now, the girl had a set of full DDDs. Hell,

I'm sure it had four Ds on it. And when we got ready to take the picture, the human in me decided to come out, and I laid my head on her chest and took the picture. I put it up on social media.

At the time, Tank had that TV show, Man Cave. I had no clue what that show was or about until somebody told me to watch it. So I did. And I was surprised to see they had a whole segment on The Cussing Pastor. According to them, I can't be a man of God because I laid my head on some titties. So, I lit into Tank's ass, and not the way he likes.

In the video, I said, "What you got against titties? Don't you like titties? So, the preacher ain't supposed to lay his head on no titties?" Then I start pulling up the receipts I had that can prove that hey, maybe he doesn't like titties. He was doing all these concerts for the gays, had them rubbing him on his legs and rubbing his chest. I said, "Oh, I see that you don't like no titties because you like dick."

If he wanted a show, I was going to give him one.

I gave them a better show than what they were trying to pull off. I noticed how boring their show was, so I sent an email to the producers. I offered to help them boost their ratings by inviting me to the show. I recommended that Tank say to me face to face what he said on the show. Get a real dialogue going. I asked for them not to edit what I'd say. I vowed not to cuss on the show but let them know that I'll still put that motherfucker in his place. And naturally, they didn't invite me to the show and well, soon after, they were gone. Sorry ass, boring ass show. That's all they needed... If I was on the show, they'd probably still be on TV.

Going Viral Was All Good

Despite what people think or feel about me, going viral has been nothing but good for me. While some negative things transpired, most of the outcome has been positive. Being on the Tosh 2.0 show ended up being a very positive experience. And honestly, it's really the only real national T.V. show that I did. And I'm glad about it because I still get checks from Tosh's show. So, it's been a very positive thing.

I know most people try to focus on the part of my brand that's not pretty or elegant, but it's effective. When I go against certain preachers in the city, it becomes positive because preachers know, "Damn if I fuck up, he's going to get me," and that's a good thing. It makes those sneaky and trifling pastors second-guess their actions.

Going viral also helped me connect with some people that I'd never consider networking with. Over the years, I've built some great relationships. One of the most unconventional friendships I've made was with TS Madison.

My relationship with her helped me connect with a Vlogger named Jason Lee. I don't know whether Jason asked her about me or told Jason about me, but T.S. contacted me and let me know that I will be hearing from Jason's people. I did hear from him. I went on the show, had a hell of a time, his numbers shot up through the roof. It shot up the roof to such a point that I've received a call from a huge production company in New York, asking me whether I wanted a T.V. show or not. So, I said, hell yeah. I told them that I don't want to do a reality show, but yeah, I want to do a talk show. So, connecting with other influencers have been very beneficial to me. I count T.S as a friend. I don't look at or judge the lifestyle of anyone. Yeah, I know when she was a porn star, but that ain't none of my business. And yes, I say 'she' because that is how she wants to be acknowledged. Who am I to say otherwise?

Okay, so I know you're thinking, "How in the hell did you get caught up with T.S. Madison?" Well, about two years ago, I had sent a message that I wanted to meet her. Eventually, she contacted me and told me she was a fan of my work as well. I went out to California to the Chateau. I did about three shows with T.S. We were scheduled to be in Mexico in 2020 together, but naturally, the pandemic halted that.

But yes, getting to know other people who are doing big things in the world helps your platform. It was a win-win situation. Her fans got to learn more about me, and my fans got to know more about her.

Before the church condemns me for being friends with T.S., Jesus hung out with worse.

As I said, I don't judge, so I'm not focused on what that person is up to when they're not working. It's not my business. When I'm on shows like that, many people find me on social media, and whether it's Facebook or Instagram, they find me and they become fans, they become followers of the show. So, it's influential to be on shows like that. I don't do shows where you don't have but ten folks watching. And I get invited to come on shows because people want me to make their show or want to have an interview with The Cussing Pastor. And I know that some folks want to attack me to see if they can get some ratings, that ain't good because I'm going to go the fuck off on you.

Like I did some little show called the Nurses of Detroit.

Now, some people may think that what I do is humorous, and that's fine, but just don't take me for a joke, and we'll be fine. I'm all for coming on your show to talk about my platform, but you won't make a mockery out of what I do, which is why I don't do shows with comedians. Usually, the comedian comes in cracking jokes and shit. I'm not a comedian. I take what I do seriously. I had an interaction on a show where a comedian tried to play me. I end up cussing him the fuck out and cussing her ass out, too. So, I don't do shows with what I call now insignificant. If there's nothing there that will benefit my brand and me, I don't do it.

People have given me flak for working with T.S., who is openly transgender, but I haven't had any negative results, so I'll keep working with her. To be honest, I've had nothing but good times. They gave me some Courvoisier, treated me real nice, flew us in, hooked me up with a nice hotel, sent a limousine to pick me up, the whole thing. But to my surprise, my learning experience came after doing the show. Her mother, Miss Mary, was cooking, oh, the kitchen was stinking up something good! The house was filled with homosexual men. No one approached me. There were no advances of any sort. Everybody there was friendly to me. And we got to talking. This was when I started to learn a thing or two. I found out that T.S. was very spiritual; her mother was very spiritual. We talked about how she gets ridiculed a lot, even by her own community. And I shared with her that she was God's perfect plan to allow the homosexual, the LGBTQ, I get them acronyms mixed up... to know that God loves the homosexual like he loves a heterosexual.

I have to be honest. I did not think I'd have such a powerful conversation with a controversial soul. At the moment, I realized I'm no different from anyone else in regards to loving God on my terms. People drag me because I cuss. Others drag homosexuals because of who they choose to give their dicks to. But we all love God, and to me, that's what matters most.

One of my most powerful words have been, in talking about homosexuals. The two words are, sissy and faggots. Now, I'm 63 years old. I come from the era when you talk about homosexuals, the word sissy was the acceptable term. When you talk about what now, people use the term lesbian, the word back in my day was bulldagger. Those were not offensive terms. So, I had known no more than what I had, but I knew faggot was disrespectful. I would say, but it was my word. And T.S. and I had a conversation about the usage of descriptive words when it comes to the homosexual community. Because of that conversation that I had with her, I don't use the word faggot anymore, and I try not to use sissies. But I think that the greatest lesson I learned is that we have to accept people for who they are and where they are in life. That's my view on that.

The Church Said What?
Now, as a Christian, I believe that we all should give people a chance to prove themselves. Unfortunately, not all. Well, most Christians don't have this mindset. So I honestly wasn't that surprised when the Church started saying things about me after finding out I'm connected to T.S. Madison.

Once the Church found out that I was in cahoots with a transgender woman, I was labeled homosexual. I was also labeled bisexual, or I was labeled ungodly. Yep, all because of a man of God that would go on a program with a homosexual. And since I wasn't ashamed of working with her, I had pictures up of T.S and me together on my platform. My arms around her, her arms around me. I knew they'd love us. That's the reason that he's on her show, to share the love.

Well, that's not how it was perceived. I was called everything but a child of God, and in true Thaddeus Matthews fashion, I cussed a few people out.

While I wasn't that shocked by their behavior, I have to admit that I found it very hypocritical for the damn Church of all places to throw shade. It kills me when the Church pretends as if they have an issue with homosexuality. They can't! Just look at all the gay choir directors, gay organ players, drummers, singers, community choirs, and even preachers. Yes, some of you have a preacher that like dick more than his wife.

I'll never understand how in the world, you want to be anti-homosexual and your Church full of homosexuals? You don't mind the homosexual coming to your Church and paying their offering, getting their tithes and money in your holier than thou Church. But then you want to get up and make a mockery out of the homosexual after you get their money.

So, I basically got to the point where I'd tell them fuck you. I'm not about to defend myself when I'm not doing anything wrong. When it comes to me, think what you want to think, think whatever is going to make you feel good, think that. My relationship with God is personal. Jesus even says, "I didn't come to condemn." So, you know, I tell them, if you like dick in your ass or in your mouth, that's your business. I ain't got nothing to do with it. If you go fuck a tree and the tree grows limbs, or the leaves start falling, I don't care. Your relationship with God is personal. Love your God.

And for those of you who want to say what the Bible says, and you mention anything about the ten commandments, well don't forget to mention what the New Testament says, and a new commandment I give unto you, to love your neighbor as yourself. So, when you talk ill against homosexuals, the transsexuals, the pansexual, or the lesbian woman, you're really talking about yourself because there is no love there. You're speaking with no love being there.

I know that a lot of the preachers, the bishops, can't tell the truth because they don't want to lose their credibility. Your favorite bishop couldn't say anything since his son came out, and honestly, none of us should say anything. See, if we got to the Church and we start dealing with homosexuality, then if God does not condemn the homosexual in the Church, how are you going to condemn the homosexual on the street?

It Is What It Is

I've learned a long time ago I'm not here to please any man. I'm here to please God. Do I get it right all the time? Fuck no. Do I keep trying? Yes, yes, I do. Many people have something to say about me and how I live my life. You know what I have to say back?

Fuck you. Very simple. If you don't feed me, finance me or fuck me and fuck me very well, I don't give a fuck what you say about me. I've grown beyond giving a damn about what you think about me. And what is your negativity about me? I can read anywhere in scripture about cursing. Now, I get people to say you curse. I said no, I don't curse. I cuss, but I don't curse. What's the difference? The difference is very simple. When I curse you, I say unto you, "You ain't shit, you ain't never gonna be shit, you didn't come from shit, your children ugly as shit, your baby going to be a little monster looking motherfucker." That's placing a curse on you. Now, when you go back and you read the scriptures, Peter cussed. Meaning, he said a word that justified his emotions.

When Jesus was in the marketplace, and he turned over the tables, you don't think Jesus cussed? Huh? Come on! I mean, he might not have had my greatest word, motherfucker, in his vocabulary. He might not have had that. But I'm sure he called people vipers. That's not a nice word for someone to be called.

Cussing is calling someone out of their name. Jesus called folk out of their names often. But some folks don't want to hear that. I know when Jesus turned the damn table, he called some folks out of their names. If Jesus had my words, he would have said, "These motherfuckers in here selling all this shit in the temple. Fuck them, I'm gonna turn this motherfucker over."

At the end of the day, whether you agree with my philosophy or deliver or not, God loves me, and I love God. I'm nothing special; just a man having a divine experience. Know that The Cussing Pastor is a man. My life is transparent. I have the same wants, desires, and needs as any other man. I like big booty women. I'll have a drink like any other man. I have the same desires. You're being called into ministry does not take the human out of you. It does not take the fact out of you that you still need God, and you still have the weaknesses of any other man. And the pretense, the bullshit from the pulpit, comes from the fact that you want to think... you want people to think that you are more than who you are. And that you don't really need God, you have already arrived. You are at the point where you're God yourself.

So, what I want people to understand about The Cussing Pastor, is that God called me for such a time as this. That April 1, 1957, on rainy Monday afternoon at 12:30 in the hospital by the name of John Gaston, that my mother, Mable-Lee Jordan, gave birth to this man of God. She had already been told of what she was carrying in her womb. That God had a mission for me that did not arrive in my early years, but he prepared me for it. In my midlife, God did not take me to the point, but he allowed me to go into radio. He allowed me to go into TV so that the name was known. He allowed me to do bold things in the community and take bold positions so that when God turned me loose as the cussing pastor, it didn't really become a surprise to me.

There are many people who will not go to church. They have been hurt and used in the church. They've been misused, they've been looked down upon, in God's house, not somebody else's house but in the house of God. They have been judged by their lifestyle, what they smoke or drink, where they've been, what they have not accomplished in life, and God is not pleased with any of that. God's design is that we all may be saved, that we all may have a reality in knowing who He is. And a lot of people will not know who God is if they're waiting on the preacher in the church because they ain't going. So, God develops a cussing pastor, the one that when you hear him, he gets your attention. He said, motherfucker, Is he a preacher? What that motherfucker said, let me listen to what that motherfucker said. When they listen to Reverend Dr. Bishop, motherfucker, they listen to me. And if they listen beyond, motherfucker, son of a bitch, shit, and all those words, they begin to get the knowledge from me that God wants them to have, not just about the Bible, but about life. Because it's more about Christ than the Bible, the 66 books do not define who God is.

In fact, the last chapter of John, in the last verse said, that if everything that was known about Jesus was written in books, there would not be enough books in the world to contain the knowledge. So, when you tell me that Jesus didn't do this, Jesus never kissed a woman, Jesus never did this. You don't know because the 66 books are Kings James's version of the Bible. This means that the version of the Bible means that this is what King James wants you to have. But you ain't told me about the lost books, you ain't told me about the Apocrypha, you ain't told me about the books of Enoch, you ain't told me about all this. You give me what? This homosexual... and when you go back and check the history of King James, King James was a homosexual.

So, how is it that the church can attack the homosexual but can believe in the book that the homosexual wrote? When you go back and look at that whiteboard that you call Jesus, whose real name was Caesar Borgia, he was the gay lover of Michael Angelo. How is it that you can look at this white boy and call him your Savior and call him your Jesus, and he's a homosexual?

One thing I understand is that people still need to come into the knowledge of who they are. And we've been forwarded this bullshit that comes from the pulpit for so long that we have been indoctrinated, and we're scared and fearful to know the truth. And the word says that you cannot be free until you know the truth. Know the truth, and the truth sets you free. That's when you understand that I can't agree with everything that's in the Bible. I can't agree with Paul. You can't tell me, Paul, to love my master. Ain't no white man, my master. I'm the master of my fate by God. I ain't going to love my enemy and my enemy, cut my head off. I'm gonna kick you in your ass if I get the chance.

When Jesus went out, Jesus went out when the 12 went out. They went out without the staff, and when they came back to Jesus, they said, Jesus them folk kind of rough out there, what we're gonna do? Jesus told them to carry their staff, which at that time was a weapon. I'm just like Jesus.

I carry my staff. It just ain't a piece of wood but a piece of steel. Praise God.

8

Bullshit From the Pulpit

O kay, so you know by now that the reason I wrote this book is that I wanted to not only expose the bullshit that these preachers are teaching at their churches. I also wanted people to know that they don't have to put up with crappy sermons and half-assed church gatherings to have a powerful connection and loving relationship with God.

So what exactly do I mean by bullshit from the pulpit? Well, it deals exactly with that with a lot of things that are going on in the church. Many people don't go to church; they left the church because the hurt in the church is the theology of a lot of these doctrines. And first of all, all of these doctrines are man-made doctrines, guarding rope; none of these doctrines are real. God didn't even write the Bible. These are doctrines, and the people who saw these doctrines before anyone else said that they started the doctrines to make themselves look good or justify them starting a new relationship.

Some years ago, I was in a meeting with a self-proclaimed Bishop. And this man's ministry was making guys here in Memphis bishops and things of that nature. For the life of me, I couldn't figure out how in the hell did they have the authority to do something they knew absolutely nothing about?

I thought to myself, what's really going on with the church? How are we just turning people into bishops, apostles, and whatever other fancy titles they've given each other over the years? What or who's authorizing these titles and positions. If now all of a sudden, this guy can walk up and tell us that this is the Full Gospel Church and these everyday men are now bishops, and what not, what have we been doing all of these years? And I said that is bullshit. We've got in the church and lost in the church that we can't even see when the wool is being pulled over our eyes. Think about it. A lot of these guys with these fancy titles, Reverend Dr. so and so, and all these letters behind their names, are just preachers. They're getting their paperwork off the computer. They've been to nobody's school. But the title is only important to them. For whatever reason, it makes them believe it helps them to look good.

They feel that people will think you are more highly than what you are because you have a piece of paper that says I'm Dr. Jones, or I'm Dr. Smith. They're excited to say, "I went to this school," and the school has been made up. Or they use real school names, but they've only been to one class. They've taken all of their stuff from a website. Didn't study a thing but have people thinking they're educated, and they're not. Just studying other people's stuff and passing it off as if it's theirs.

So, when we look at bullshit from the pulpit, that's what I'm referring to. I think many people are misleading the people of God. We're not taught many things about the truth. Even going way back with the name of the Messiah, Jesus. There was no letter J in the Hebrew or the Greek language around that era. So that means that the name for Jesus would have been Yahushua. But the name Jesus is the name that is using it, and people are comfortable with that. But if we know our history, then we know where the bullshit is. When you look at the factor of the whiteboard, you call Jesus.

The image they are passing around as Jesus was a homosexual by the name of Caesar Borgia. Yet, the church that says anti-homosexual studies makes their God a homosexual. Now, that doesn't make any sense at all! It's hard to teach people the truth when they have been pacified with such a potent lie. Truth is, many Christians don't even know who Jesus is. Your Scripture says he had hair like lamb's wool, feet like brass, eyes like balls of fire, but you worship this whiteboard with this nice hair and pretty blue eyes. And you say that this is your Lord and Savior that you die to be in the presence of this gay white sissy... Bullshit!

You study a book that's called the King James Version of the Bible. This means this is what he wants to have, not God. He leaves out the rest of the stuff. A man decided that 66 books are enough for you to read about God and the Messiah.

King James was a homosexual. According to the records. King James not only wrote the Bible, but he also wrote a book on demonology. So, you get this guy that can give you Jesus in a handbasket. But not only does he give you Jesus, but he also gives you demons and things of that nature. I say it's bullshit.

You hear men saying God called them. They heard a voice at night while sleeping that said, "Preach." Bullshit.

The first black preacher wasn't documented until we got here in 1619, from the Ivory Coast of Africa on the slave ship. The first slave ship was entitled The Good Ship Jesus when you sail from Africa to this land on the good ship Jesus. And the white man indoctrinated you. He indoctrinated you with what you call Christianity. He took your religion from you; he took your name from you. Hell, the white man takes your God and your belief away. And he indoctrinates you with what he wants you to say. You know black men, you weren't supposed to read. So, everything the black preacher stated back in those days was what the white man indoctrinated him to say. Give a Negro piece of chicken, and that Negro going to whoop and holler and tell people exactly what the white man says. And the black man finds himself in a box. We're in a box of ignorance because this is what we have been taught to our people for hundreds of years.

We were taught to trust what the white man says about God. To trust the part where he tells us about Paul. And Paul tells you to obey your master. In fact, the white man indoctrinated the black preacher to be able to control the slaves. Well, you know God doesn't want you to go against your master. And that's what I call bullshit from the pulpit.

Not allowing folks to come into the church because of how they look, the way they dress, and their socio-economic conditions. Bullshit.

Not allowing people from the streets, gang members, whores, and prostitutes or crooks to come into the church to help them deal with their bullshit is bullshit.

If God allows everybody to come before Him, how does the church say that you can't go to the place where you're supposed to get to know more about Him?

Are Pastors *Really* Called to Preach?

One of the things I continuously call bullshit on is when men say they were called to preach. Can a man be called to preach? Well, the inspiration does come from God. But while hearing those scientific voices, there is a propelling of your spirit by God, that you need to go out and minister to these people. We're all ministers. Everybody's a minister. Some take off as an occupation, takes it on as a leading role. But there is something that is stirred up in you by God that tells you that you are supposed to be up there with those people.

The pastor is an individual desert preacher as I was in my teen years, who left the church who came back because of my mother's death. But it was all a part of God's plan because it propelled me into the avenue and the place that I am. Because these weak preachers are scared to deal with the people in specific industries, they're too weak to tell them the truth. God has me in place to do such a thing to go into clubs and preach and go everywhere. And preaching is not whooping and hollering. Preaching is not taking a text. The word gospel means good news. So, if I'm sharing with you the good news of life, that's a sermon.

Corruption in the Church

Who would have thought that you'll find corruption in the very place that you're supposed to find Christ? Well, it happens. The church is one of the most corrupt institutions around, and that's some straight-up bullshit.

Another thing I call bullshit on is how churches beg for tithes and offerings. Well, when you read one of the most significant scriptures, that uses Malachi 3:10, will a man rob God? When you read that chapter and read the holiness of the third chapter, you will find out that the chapter is not about the people giving. But it's about the priests and those who are over the storehouse, to watch the storehouse. And that day, you have to bring your tithes or bring your chickens or whatever it was that you consider your 10th. It was brought to them for everybody in the community.

I give because I believe in being blessed. The most positive scripture in the Bible is one that many use negatively. You're going to reap what you sow. I give because the Bible says, be not deceived. That means don't be fooled. But God is not mocked. He's not lying. Then the next word is very vital: whatsoever. In other words, whatsoever a man sow is what will be planted. The next word says that shall he also reap. So, if I plant some money, or positiveness that's what will come back to me. And I believe that God pays with interest.

To be clear, my issue isn't the church asking people to give; it's that the church don't give back to the people. In 2019, $18 billion was raised in the black church. How many hospitals did we build in our community? How many neighborhoods did we build? Or did those $18 billion go back into banks and go into the officers of churches? What are we doing with the money in the church? No one can ever answer this question, and that's some bullshit.

If you went all day to church, and when you get out of the church, you can't even buy a box of Church's Chicken, you in the wrong place in the first place. The preacher must also learn to preach more about just going to heaven and that you will see mom and 'nem over yonder. The preacher has got to learn to preach about prosperity and abundance. It's the way of life for people. And because this isn't being taught, the people are struggling and tithing the wrong way. Scripture says, the enemy comes to kill, steal, and destroy, but I come that you may have life and have that life more abundantly. How will the people live abundantly if they're not being taught how?

Know the Truth and Be Free
It's about time for preachers to really stop with the lies and start teaching the truth. The next issue I can bullshit on in the church is that they teach one-sided things. I also believe that this is why people

need to find the truth on their own outside of the church and what they're grandmothers have passed down. While there is a lot of great information in the Bible, there is a lot of misinformation. And when I say misinformation, it's information missing out of the book. And many people will tell you that if the King James Version doesn't say it, it can't be right. And I beg to differ with that. You need to read more than just the King James Version of the Bible. You should read the books of Enoch, the Apocrypha, the laws books of the Bible. In the book of John, the very last chapter in the previous verse says, if everything that Jesus had done had been written in books, that would not be enough books in the world that could contain everything that Jesus did.

Remember now - eighteen years are missing out on the Life of Christ in the King James Version of the Bible. You see him at twelve. He didn't come back until thirty. Where was Jesus that those eighteen years? What did Jesus do in those eighteen years? Yet, the church will tell you that ain't important.

Actually, it's vital! We all need to know what Jesus was doing. He wasn't around. But why is that being not important to the preacher? Because he doesn't know. So, saying he doesn't know now means that he has to do some research. Well, he's too lazy for that, so he'll just say that you don't need that part. Forget about that. Just do what the Bible says to do.

See, this is all bullshit that most preachers know and won't say anything about because we've been taught not to speak out against the church. It's blasphemy.

Unfortunately, people have been taught to put the church on this unrealistic pedestal. They have been taught that you're not supposed to think for yourself. The pastor does your thinking for you. When it comes to heaven and things, you don't think yourself. Just believe whatever the preacher says. God called him, so he knows. And that's the reason I think a lot of people don't reach out to God for themselves. Plus, they don't read for themselves. They go to church out of habit and have no clue what's really going on. Many people refuse to read for themselves, study for themselves, or find out what meanings of words mean in the scriptures that the pastor is reading. This is what I believe keeps people stuck in their mess. They have no real understanding of the truth.

Good thing is, it's not too late for the church to turn this negative narrative around. First, the church has to change its current mindset. The leaders have to humble themselves and admit that there are some things they don't know and go out and learn them.

Too many leaders want to continue to con and bamboozle their congregation. They're okay with giving people the wrong information, sweating a little bit, mesmerizing the people for 30 or 40 minutes, and then when he's done, he goes into his office. Then to his car, then to his big house with your tithes and offerings, and will see you next Sunday to do it all over again.

If you are stuck at these types of churches with these types of pastors, two words: Get out. Go to a church where you can learn something that will lead you to true wholeness and abundance because that's what God wants for you. Understand this - there is no perfect religion of perfect denomination. Every denomination has issues, but that doesn't mean you have to sit under a corrupt ministry. Don't be lazy about your spiritual journey. Ask questions to make sure you're at the right place. What is the church doing? What's the pastor doing for the membership? What is he doing for the community? How many offerings do they take up on a Sunday? Is there more emphasis on finances than on the information that people need in the church? Or is the pastor spending any time with you? Is it all about the money and all about his time? What is he doing for you as a pastor? Can you talk to your pastor, or do you have to talk to a mediator before going to your next pastor?

So, I think that there has to be a desire to turn around. And I don't believe that in many churches, that there is any desire to make a turnaround because they're comfortable where they are.

9

Thaddy Daddy

Among the many hats that I wear, the most adventurous hat for me is the fatherhood hat. I have four kids, and I can admit that I haven't been the best father over the years. To be honest, my relationship with my children has been strained over the years, but we're okay now. I was that father that was not around and didn't have a father myself. It may sound cliché or immature, but the truth is I didn't know how to be a father. I didn't know about the provisions of taking care of children. Just the understanding of how to make children. I had no one to teach me what a man was supposed to do. As far as being a father was concerned. And everything that I've gathered, everything that I learned, I learned it from the streets. And somethings I learned from the street just weren't right. But now I'm a whole different person.

For years, my relationship with my oldest daughter, Jocelyn, was strained. For many years, I was not there; I wasn't around. Sometimes I don't think she ever forgave me for not being around. But we're working on that. Then my next child would be my oldest son. A drunk driver killed him.

His name was Kenya Matthews. Our relationship was okay. It could have been a lot better. And my last two kids are ghetto twins! Don't you judge me now! But it's my truth. They were born a month apart. Yes, I had two different women pregnant. I was married and I had an affair. I got the girl pregnant and my wife was pregnant too. Both of the children are about a month apart. So, I've been down that road. Thank God I never have to travel that road again!

My son, whose name is Raymond Matthews. Our relationship was strained for a while. He worked for me for a time in the repo business. Then he came back and decided we should be hunky-dory and all in fine. And I'm okay with that.

Then I have my baby daughter, Dominic Matthews. This is the daughter that's going to check on her daddy. This is the daughter that notices if I need anything. She checks on me and does all the daddy-daughter things. So, those are the four children that I have.

As I mentioned, being a father did not come naturally to me. It was something that I learned by fucking up trying to be a father to my kids. It took me a while, but finally, I understand what the role of a father is.

A father is to be strong. Yes, being a provider and providing is good when they're small, but there's more to it than that. What do we do when they're grown? Because I don't believe in taking care of grown folk. So, this is where having wisdom as a father is important. After they're full and grown, they still need your presence. Not to tell them what to do, but to nurture them. Nurturing them is giving them enlightenment and wisdom. Providing information, they'll need to make it in this world. Being that voice or be the ear that they can call on. That's the proper role of a father.

For the fathers who feel it's too late because their kids are grown, change that mindset. It's never too late to build a relationship with your kids. Just know that it's going to take some effort. Make contact, make the call first. The hardest thing for a man to do when he has not been in his child's life is to make contact with a child because there is a fear of the unknown. There's a fear of whether or not this child is going to accept you or not. In many cases, you're not accepted and that hurts. So, men avoid the call altogether to avoid being hurt.

Then, what if that person does not want to hear from you? Now that man is dealing with rejection. And we all know by now that men handle rejection a lot harder than women. But this is no excuse. It's just a few reasons why fathers who aren't around don't reach out. For the men who are courageous enough to face that fear, know that you've got to be big enough to say to your children, "Look, I made a mistake, I fucked up. Are you willing to give me another chance?"

If you want to be in your kids' lives, whether their small children or adults, that's what you have to do. You have to humble yourself and go and seek your children. Not being there is one of my deepest regrets. Let's break this cycle.

You may think, well, Thaddeus, how can we break this cycle? Now, this may sound crazy, but follow me. Before you have a child, make sure that you know the woman you get with. Get scientific on that ass. Make sure that the DNA is going to mix as far as making a triangle. You need to know that. What is their mindset like? What are some traits they inherited from their people? These things matter. You don't want to be the one with a Ph.D., and you get with somebody that dropped out of school in the second grade. I don't know whether that child will be dumb or smart. You're going to be fucked up one way or the other. If you're great at money management, don't impregnate a woman who only sees dollar signs. Do you want an athletic child? Marry a woman who was a track star in high school. Just do your due diligence before you plant your send in the womb of a woman who doesn't have what it takes to properly nurture your seed.

Now, I'm going to say something that most women will find offensive, but it's the truth. I believe that fatherhood is a thing that most men are not looking for unless you're married. You're not looking really for fatherhood when you're a single man. You just had plans to get some good sex, and it happened. Whether that's your truth or not, it's not the children's fault. You may not have signed up for a baby, but now he/she is here. So, what I say is, love your kids, be there for your kids. And that's all you can do. Don't be upset with the woman for having the baby. Just have a mature conversation. Decide to co-parent with her. Be present in your kids' lives. Let them know you care. Build a relationship with them. Allow them to get to know you, so you don't have their mother saying lies about you to them.

Being a father is a blessing no matter how the child is conceived. Remind yourself that you're assigned to a role that is one of the most critical parts of anyone's life. Boys and girls need their father, so be present, show up, even when it's hard. Remember, it's not just about money. Focus on building a personal relationship with your children so that you can always stay connected to them no matter what.

10

It Ain't Ova

Now that you know a little more about The Cussing Pastor, I hope that you can look past the cussing and dive into the message of this book. I hope that you can look past my ratchet and wretched ways and acknowledge me as a man who loves God, women, and cussing. Whether you agree with my choice of words or not, know that I'm proud of the man I've become. I don't let anyone else's thoughts direct my path, and I've successfully created a life that makes me happy and that I thoroughly enjoy living.

I have to admit that I'm most proud of myself. My accomplishments in broadcasting are enough for me to be proud of alone. I started at a little station called WXSS. I have worked very hard to be at the level that I am right now. I've never been in school, never taken a course for broadcasting. It's my God-given ability. I'm proud of my years on TV, and I'm looking to be proud of whatever is next for me. I think that there is something way out of my realm of thinking set before me.

In my mind, I've mastered radio, next I'd like to master national television. I'm looking to be everywhere on TV. I'll talk about similar topics that are on my radio show. But of course, I'll have to clean it up since my radio show is unfiltered. I don't mind putting on a little filter for TV. Just know that this is the beginning of The Cussing Pastor. There is much more wisdom, knowledge, and life lessons that I want to share. There are more people that I want to serve, talk to, support, guide, and help. I've been walking this earth for over six decades. I have a lot to give and share, and now I'm ready.

Has It All Been Worth It?

Now, before I go, I have to share with you the top three lessons I've learned becoming a man and The Cussing Pastor. The first lesson I've learned is patience. And can I be real? This is not something that I've had as a younger man. I learned about this virtue the hard way, as most people do. If I can offer some advice on this: understand that nothing comes easy or overnight. And it's not about why or the time you wait, but the posture in which you wait. Stay grateful and mentally ready for what you're asking for.

Let's see, the second lesson I want to share is that you can be whatever you want to be. If you apply yourself to it, do the hard work, you can be whatever you want to be. I had no clue that I'd have a platform that would impact the lives of so many. Some negative, but mostly positive.

And the third thing I've learned is survival. I've survived the hardships of life that most people break from. I've mastered resilience. Resilience is the key to help you accomplish anything. So yeah, that was a great lesson.

There's not much that I'd change about my journey. If I could go back and look at some of the mistakes that I made in the broadcasting business years ago, I would probably change some of them. But I wouldn't change myself. I wouldn't change my language, but I might change the way I dealt with some people over the years.

You know, I'm a very blunt person. When somebody pisses me off, it's nothing to tell them to just kiss my ass. I've spoken sometimes out of turn to people when it wasn't really necessary. Well, maybe it was necessary, but my delivery was all wrong. Whether right or wrong, I'm grateful for this journey that I traveled. I've made a lot of friends, and I made a lot of enemies in this business. But through it all, I've survived.

The best thing I did for myself was I learned as much as I can about the radio industry on my own. Take it from me, don't depend on anybody else to teach you a craft. Take the time to research the ins and outs of the industry you plan to dominate. You have to care enough about your success. So, do what is necessary to be successful in your business.

Understanding The Cussing Pastor

I know that most pastors pretend as if they don't cuss, but I don't. I know that most pastors pretend to be this meek and mild man of God, but I'm very transparent and very blunt about who I am. I have a 'don't give a fuck' attitude, and I still love God. I've learned to say no, and I'm still giving and caring when I want to be. I used to be just a captain save-a-hoe. Now, these hoes got to save themselves!

Now, I'll never expect anyone to accept things about me that make them uncomfortable. However, I hope that whether or not you are comfortable with the things that I say, you have a better understanding of who The Cussing Pastor is. Whether you believe me or not, there's nothing more important to me than my ministry and my brand. So that's what I'm working on. That's where I want to be. That's what I'm going to do.

About the Author

Thaddeus Augustus Matthews was born in Memphis, TN, on April Fool's day. Mr. Matthews was called into the ministry at an early age. After years of participating and subjecting himself to the traditional rituals of the church, he left the fold. He didn't attend church for a number of years before returning, only after promising his mother he would.

Mr. Matthews is most famous for his time on Memphis radio as the well-known "Shock Jock"! He was first introduced to the field in 1985. After several years on the radio, Thaddeus created his own television show, The Thaddeus Matthews TV Show. He has received over 100 plaques and awards for his style, technique and reporting ongoing events to the community.

Currently, the charismatic thought-leader now pastors the Naked Truth Liberation and Empowerment Ministries. This is not your grandmother's church! In the last four years, the ministry has contributed to the community in multiple ways. Mr. Matthews has a very hands-on approach to the community through outreach. He holds events at the church to help all walks of life.

During one of his online outreach events, one of the viewers confronted him. He cussed her out and was given the moniker, The Cussing Pastor. Mr. Matthews, aka The Cussing Pastor, is also a social media icon. He has several thousand followers on Facebook, Instagram and YouTube.

Made in the USA
Columbia, SC
28 February 2021